My New Life
Vision Board Clip Art Book
For Women

I have been making vision boards for a long time, and over the years, it has become a birthday ritual. Each year o my birthday I create a vision board for the year ahead. This personal experience and passion for vision boards inspired me to create this book.

Based on my own experience, I have organized this book into categories that will help you to envision a holistic future. There are little tips and write-ups for each category that might be useful as you organize your own thoughts. Of course, you may not always find the exact picture you are looking for, but this book will help you to create a basic board. You can keep embellishing your board by adding other pictures or quotes that you may come across.

My top tip for you is to let your intuition guide you in this creative process. If an image grabs your attention then just add it to your board, my experience has taught me that the subconscious is far more powerful than the conscious mind so let it guide you.

Don't let the sections restrict your selection of an image, they're there just as a guideline so you don't miss out on an important aspect of your life.

Another suggestion is that always look at your vision board with optimism and the belief that the Universe is hard at work making happen for you. Please do not look at your board wondering when this will happen or even worse focus on what is right now missing in your life. Remember the Law of Attraction responds to your emotions not your thoughts, so if the lack of these things is what you emotionally project, then that is exactly what you will attract.

Please do leave a review on Amazon so that I can incorporate your feedback into the next book.

I hope you enjoy creating your new life!

Sualeha

Health & Wellness

In this section you will find pictures related to the following:

Eating Healthy

Hydration

Exercise

Meditate

Relax

Be Free

Our mind envisions the future but our body is the vessel we need to achieve it. Therefore, taking care of our bodies is the key to fulfilling our goals and desires. Health is not merely physical fitness nor is it weight loss - they are one aspect of it. Your mind is part of your body so what are you doing to take care of it? Are you sleeping well? Are you able to spend some time just relaxing and not dwelling on the past, present or worrying about the future? If you could achieve whatever you wanted will you be able to enjoy it physically?

Food Journal

Start Date:
Start Weight:
Target Weight:

Measurements at Start

Chest:
Waist:
Hips:
Thighs:
Upper Arms:
BMI:

#TAKE CARE OF YOURSELF

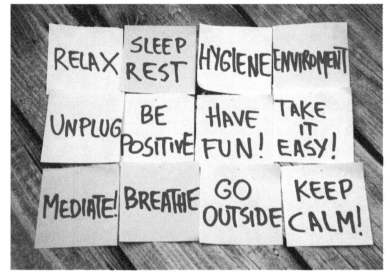

RELAX | SLEEP REST | HYGIENE | ENVIRONMENT
UNPLUG | BE POSITIVE | HAVE FUN! | TAKE IT EASY!
MEDIATE! | BREATHE | GO OUTSIDE | KEEP CALM!

enjoy the little things

SLEEP WELL

LIVING
IN
FREEDOM
EVERYDAY

Relationships

The pictures in this section can be grouped as"
Couples
Family & Children
Siblings & Friends

What good is success without friends and family with whom to share it with? Our relationships are the glue that keeps our life together, without loved ones we become 'undone' very quickly. What kind of relationships do you want in your life? Are there any relationships that need a bit more attention? Is there a relationship that you need to work on? Who are the people you are grateful for in your life? Are you showing gratitude towards these people?

Rather than focusing on 'who' you want to share your life with focus on 'what' kind of person you want to share it with.

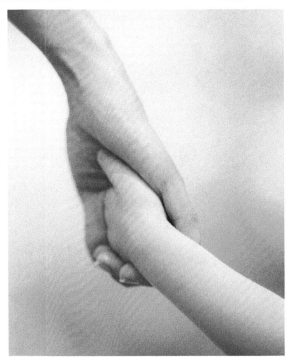

Career

What do you want to do? Where does your passion lie? What is your unique talent? Success is more than just making a paycheck. After all, if you are dying of boredom and feel stuck in a job, will you have the zest left in you to enjoy success when it finally comes?

Personal Growth

Growth comes from stepping out of your comfort zone, taking on challenges and facing life's problems head-on. Make learning and growing your primary purpose in life. What are the lessons life is trying to teach you right now? Is there someone in your life that makes you feel really low? If so, then ask yourself why you feel this way and what behaviours you need to change or develop to stop reacting this way. What triggers you and how you can change yourself to make these triggers neutral? Remember all events are neutral, how we react tp them makes them good or bad. Do you need to improve your knowledge and skills to be able to achieve your career goals?

Always Room to Grow

GET THE CREATIVITY FLOWING

Learn Something New Everyday

Fuel Your Passion

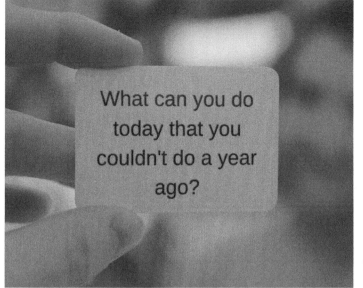

What can you do today that you couldn't do a year ago?

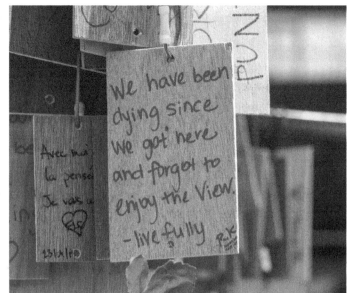

We have been dying since we got here and forgot to enjoy the View.
- live fully

MY BRAIN HAS TOO MANY TABS OPEN

WORRY LESS

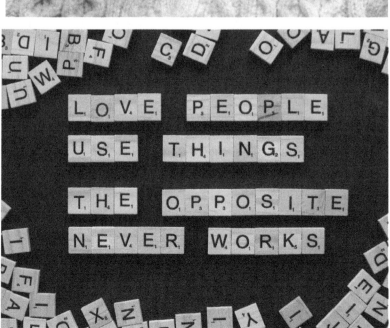

LOVE PEOPLE, USE THINGS, THE OPPOSITE, NEVER WORKS.

Financial Abundance

This section is dedicated to money and symbols of wealth. If you want financial abundance then you first have to get comfortable with money. Why will the Universe give you something that makes you uncomfortable? What is the figure you want in your account?

Success

What will you do with your financial abundance? Money is just a means to get things or fulfil desires so how will you use your wealth? Everyone's definition of success is different - how would you define your success? If you don't know what success means to you then how would you know if you have achieved it or not?

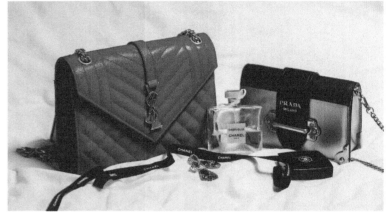

Travel & Adventure

What kind of experiences will you have when you are successful? Where do you want to go? How would you like to get there? Remember life is nothing but a series of experiences so what experiences will you like to have?

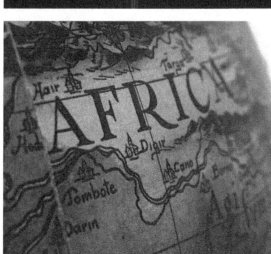

Nature

Nature heals and soothes the spirit. Spend some time being close to it and renew yourself.

Spirit

Take some 'me time' and calm yourself. Strengthen your bond with this Universe, let go of your worries and nourish your spirit through meditation, quiet reflection or prayer. Remember "when you let go - that's when things flow".

FAITH
can move
MOUNTAINS
MATTHEW 17:20

Hobbies

I can't stress enough the importance of having a hobby. Hobbies lift our moods and help take our minds off our worries. We get so absorbed in them that we forget about our goals, dreams and desires, allowing the Universe to manifest them. Remember the more we worry about getting what we want the more resistance which in turn delays our manifestations.

Obviously, there are so many hobbies that we cannot cover even a small percentage of them, but this section is there to remind you to revive an old hobby or pick a new one.

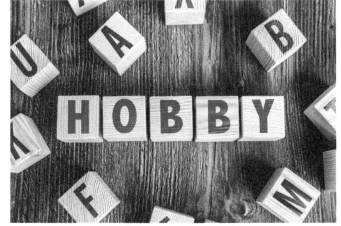

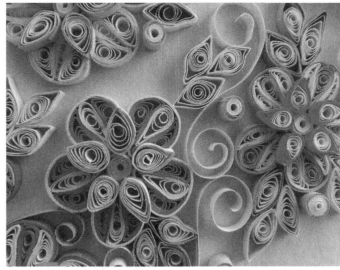

Miscellaneous

This section has random pictures to spark your imagination. Personally I use such images metaphorically rather than literally.

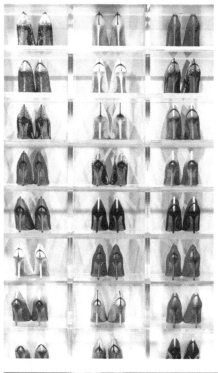

Some People
Cause Happiness

Wherever
They Go

Others Whenever
They Go

To Avoid
Criticism

Do Nothing
Say Nothing
Be Nothing

The Future
Belongs To Those
Who Believe
In The Beauty
Of Their Dreams

Most people
would rather be
CERTAIN they are
MISERABLE
than risk
being **HAPPY**

The secret of **SUCCESS**
is to do the
common things
UNCOMMONLY well!

There is NO future
in any JOB
the future lies
in the PERSON
who holds the job!

LET'S
START THE
JOURNEY
——>>>

Made in the USA
Monee, IL
18 October 2023

44686995R00070